THE presence OF peace

LLOYD
JOHN
OGILVIE

Paintings by

H
HARVEST HOUSE™ PUBLISHERS

EUGENE, OREGON

THE presence of peace

Text Copyright © 2002 by Lloyd John Ogilvie

Published by Harvest House Publishers

Eugene, Oregon 97402

ISBN 0-7369-1023-9

Media Arts Group, Inc.

900 Lightpost Way

Morgan Hill, CA 95037

1.800.366.3733

Text from this book previously appeared in *Perfect Peace* by Lloyd John Ogilvie (Harvest House Publishers, 2001) and *Quiet Moments with God* by Lloyd John Ogilvie (Harvest House Publishers, 1997)

Design and production by Koechel Peterson and Associates, Minneapolis, Minnesota

Printed in Hong Kong.

02 03 04 05 06 07 08 09 10 11 / NG / 10 9 8 7 6 5 4 3 2 1

peace
in our hearts

begins with
Christ's
healing love.

The PRESENCE of PEACE

UE PEACE IS WHOLENESS—mental health, emotional stability, volitional integration, and physical well-being. When this quality of peace reigns in you, it cannot be debilitated by people or circumstances. True peace cannot be broken by life's storms...and actually grows deeper with the challenges and trials of life.

Peace does not dwell in outward things, but in the heart prepared to wait trustfully and quietly on him who has all things safely in his hands.

ELISABETH ELLIOT

Thank You for this time of quiet with You in which I can receive the peace of knowing that I am loved and forgiven, the healing of the hurts of harbored memories, the answers to problems that often seem unsolvable, and the vision for solutions that otherwise would be beyond any human understanding. I praise You that to know You is my greatest joy and to serve You is life's greatest delights.

HERE IS ONLY ONE source of consistent peace—God. The peace of God is His unrivaled authority. There is no real peace without a firm conviction of the sovereignty of God!

God's superlative peace is given to those whose minds are intentionally riveted on Him. We must keep our minds stayed on God.

In Thy will is our Peace.

DANTE

It is not because things are difficult that we do not dare; it is because we do not dare that things are difficult.

SENECA

May Your peace invade my heart so my attitude will reflect an inner serenity and calm confidence.

The shams of life may rage around you, but inside there will be calm because you can pray in the midst of uncertainties, conflict, turmoil, and adversity. Prayer will stay your mind on God and fill your thoughts with His peace.

Shod my feet with the preparation
of the gospel of peace
and help me to stride forward
with the inner calm
of Your perfect peace,
which surpasses all understanding.

When peace like a river attendeth my way,
When sorrows like sea billows roll;
Whatever my lot, Thou hast taught me to say,
It is well, it is well with my soul.

HORATIO SPAFFORD

Be of good comfort, be of one
mind, live in peace; and the
God of love and peace
will be with you.

2 CORINTHIANS 13:11

BEDIENCE TO WHAT GOD reveals in our daily and moment-by-moment prayers is the secret to lasting peace.

Grace is God's gift to us. We could not live a day without a fresh supply of it. Fitting grace, grace that is suited to our specific needs, the grace of Jesus Christ always brings peace.

gratitude

.ACE AND PRAISE go together. There's a renewed, fresh gift of peace in gratitude.

Real success in life means living without the worry, fretting, or care that comes from trying to control everything ourselves.

Every tomorrow has two handles. We can take hold of it by the handle of anxiety, or by the handle of faith.

SOURCE UNKNOWN

Peace I leave with you, my peace I give to you…Let not your heart be troubled.

John 14:27

Grant me this day a profound sense of Your peace—

a true peace that comes from complete trust

in You and dependence on Your guidance.

PEACE IS FORGIVENESS. Peace is trusting. Peace is giving our worries over to Christ and leaving the results to Him.

God's peace is available to you and me today. Peace can be ours as soon as we begin living with the assurance that God's intervention will come on time, in time, and in the right way. We need only pray as Christ did, clearly acknowledging our dependence upon the Father.

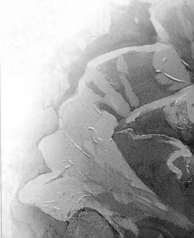

You will go out in joy and be led forth in peace; the mountains and hills will burst into song before you, and all the trees of the field will clap their hands.

ISAIAH 55:12

Meanwhile, beneath thy gracious sight
This flock has dwelt in peace and light,
By living waters gently led,
And in perennial pastures fed.

WILLIAM CULLEN BRYANT

A contemporary rendering of the Twenty-Third Psalm

The Lord is my strength,

I shall not panic;

He helps me relax and rest

in quiet trust.

He reminds me that I belong to Him

and restores my serenity;

He leads me in my decisions and gives

me calmness of mind.

His presence is peace.

Even though I walk through the valley

of the fear of failure,

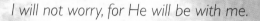

I will not worry, for He will be with me.

His truth, grace, and lovingkindess
will stabilize me.

He prepares release and renewal
in the midst of my stress.

He anoints my mind with wisdom;

My cup overflows with fresh energy.

Surely goodness and mercy will be
communicated through me,

For I shall walk in the strength of my Lord,

And dwell in His presence forever. Amen.

Submit to God and be at peace with him; in this way prosperity will come to you.

JOB 22:21

VE YOUR PROBLEMS to God. Do it today! You'll be on your way to deeper peace than you've ever experienced.

Perfect peace cannot be contrived by our understanding alone.

Oh, let thy peace, the peace that tames
The wayward heat, inhabit here,
That quenches passion's fiercest flames,
And thaws the deadly frost of fear.

WILLIAM CULLEN BRYANT

The achievement of your goal is assure
the moment you commit yourself to it

MACK R. DOUGLAS

HE PEACE of God is the Spirit of Christ. His shalom, harmony, wholeness, well-being, and knitting together of what is fragmented or frayed in us comes to us when we invite Christ to dwell in our hearts and minds.

Provider of Peace, give me the peace of a cleansed
and committed heart, a free and forgiving heart,
a caring and compassionate heart.
May Your deep peace flow into me,
calming my impatience and flowing from me
to others claiming Your inspiration.

Like a river glorious, is God's perfect peace,
Over all victorious in its bright increase;
Perfect yet it floweth fuller every day;
Perfect yet it groweth deeper all the way.

FRANCES HAVERGAL

CHRIST GIVES US strength to let go of our tight grip on our worries, commit them to Him, and open ourselves to an inflow of fresh peace.

May the serenity and peace I feel at this moment sustain me throughout this day.
I thank You, in advance, for a great day filled with incredible surprises of sheer joy.

GOD WORKS THINGS OUT. Things don't just work out.

Calm soul of all things! make it mine

To feel, amid the city's jar,

That there abides a peace of thine,

Man did not make, and cannot mar!

The will to neither strive nor cry,

The power to feel with others give!

Calm, calm me more! nor let me die

Before I have begun to live.

MATTHEW ARNOLD

Jesus, the calm that fills my breast,
No other heart than Thine can give;
This peace unstirred, this joy of rest,
None but Thy loved ones can receive.

FRANK NORTH

IS TIMES OF PAIN that our Lord saves—heals to the uttermost.

And that includes the pain you are experiencing right now.

Don't just endure it. Invite the Lord to invade every part of

your being with His peace.

The Lord gives strength to
his people; the Lord blesses
his people with peace.

PSALM 29:11

Lovely, lasting peace of mind!
Sweet delight of human-kind!
Heavenly-born, and bred on high,
To crown the fav'rites of the sky
With more of happiness below,
Than victors in a triumph know!
Whither, O whither art thou fled,
To lay thy meek, contented head;
What happy region dost thou please
To make the seat of calms and ease!

Lovely, lasting peace, appear!
This world itself, if thou art here,
Is once again with Eden blest,
And man contains it in his breast.

THOMAS PARNELL
"A HYMN TO CONTENTMENT"

I claim Isaiah's promise, "You will keep him
in perfect peace whose mind
is stayed on You" (Isaiah 26:3 NKJV).
Stay my mind on You so I may know
Your lasting peace of mind and soul.

You never will be the person you can be if
pressure, tension and discipline are taken
out of your life.

JAMES G. BILKEY

PEACE IS NOT NEAR, but here—within. It's not only Christ with us, but Christ in us. Peace is more than a state of freedom from jangled nerves; more than transient harmony, a temporary truce in relationships; more than a transitory calm in the storms of life. The peace of Christ is His own peace.

Peace grows in the fertile soil of a relinquished will.

Loosen my tight grip on everything and everyone. I open the floodgates of my mind and heart so I can receive Your serenity.

What makes humility so desirable is the marvelous thing it does to us; it creates in us a capacity for the closest possible intimacy with God.

MONICA BALDWIN

PEACE PRODUCES AN active, confident trust that the Lord is on time, in time, and never one moment ahead of time for our times. Patience is knowing that the Lord has ruled what is best for us and that we will have it in His perfect timing. Peace is patience.

I do not ask to walk smooth paths
Nor bear an easy load.
I pray for strength and fortitude
To climb the rock-strewn road.

Give me such courage I can scale
The hardest peaks alone,
And transform every stumbling block
Into a stepping-stone.

Gail Brook Burket

There comes to my heart one sweet
strain, a glad and a joyous refrain;

I sing it again and again, sweet peace,
the gift of God's love.

Peace, peace, sweet peace!
Wonderful gift from above!

Oh, wonderful, wonderful peace! Sweet
peace, the gift of God's love!

PETER BILHORN

WHEN PEACE RESIDES in our hearts we can be peacemakers. We can become the initial reconcilers of conflict.

Thank You for setting me free

from any burdens of worry and anxiety

so I can remain focused on the challenges

and decisions I face today.

I claim Your promises to give me

strength that endures,

peace in the pressures,

light for the way, wisdom for the choices,

and love for those whom I meet today.

TRUE PEACE IS MAINTAINED when we can affirm that we have lived out our eternal goal in the midst of our daily stresses. A good day ending with profound inner peace is a day in which we have fought the good fight, run the race, and kept the faith.

There are many things that are essential to arriving at true peace of mind, and one of the most important is faith, which cannot be acquired without prayer.

JOHN WOODEN

The morning breaks,
  And warm and bright
The earth lies still
  In the golden light—
For Dawn has scattered the clouds of night.

God's handiwork
  Is seen around,
Things great and small
  To his praise abound—
Where are the signs of his love not found?

All things must pass,
  But God shall still
With steadfast power
  His will fulfill—
Sure and unshaken is His will.

His saving grace
  Will never fail,
Though grief and fear
  The heart assail—
O'er life's wild seas he will prevail.

Joy shall be ours
  In that garden blest,
Where after storm
  We find our rest—
I wait in peace—God's time is best.

                    JOHANNA SPYRI

Troubles are often the tools by which God fashions us for better things.

HENRY WARD BEECHER